NANDILYN WILLIAMS

LION *of* JUDAH

ROAR *in* ME

CREATION
HOUSE

LION OF JUDAH, ROAR IN ME by Nandilyn Williams
Published by Creation House
A Strang Company
600 Rinehart Road
Lake Mary, Florida 32746
www.creationhouse.com

Scripture quotations are from the New King James Version of the Bible. Copyright © 1979, 1980, 1982 by Thomas Nelson, Inc., publishers. Used by permission.

Cover design by Rachel Campbell

Library of Congress Control Number: 2006929487
International Standard Book Number: 1-59979-074-2

First Edition

06 07 08 09 10 — 987654321
Printed in the United States of America

This book by my friend is strong, strong, strong, very readable, and exceptionally timely. Reading this book is a powerful experience. I trust you will let as many new and powerful ideas from the Word get a hold of you. Your life is worth it!

—DR. BARBARA GUTHRIE
FOUNDER, DISCOVERING DIRECTIONS FOR LIFE
CHRISTIAN COUNSELING CENTER

Lion of Judah, Roar in Me will inspire Christians to take a stand and proclaim their faith with renewed energy and commitment. Its message is one that we all need to be reminded of from time to time.

—KENDRA CHRISTOPHER
PRESIDENT, LIGHTWISE DESIGN

To every man, woman, and teenager who dares to rise up from slumber and self-absorption to understand the Word of God, and demand that the will of the Lord be done.

Acknowledgment

For every trial and hindrance, I thank You for pushing me to the foot of the cross. It was worth it!

CONTENTS

Preface...xi

Foreword... 1

1 *Jesus, My Strength* 7

2 *Courage, Confidence, and Fearlessness*...................... 17

3 *Attack First* 25

4 *The Lion of Judah* 33

5 *It Is Time to Roar*...39

6 *What Really Matters* 45

PREFACE

*L*ION OF JUDAH, ROAR IN ME gives answers to the complexities of life that have many of us wondering why life is what it is, so boring and unfulfilling. Throughout the body of Christ and the world there is an overwhelming spirit of discontentment and displacement causing many to drift through life never fulfilling their God-given purpose. Unfortunately, many of us think our God-inspired dreams will just unfold one day, without any effort on our part, but that is not the case. It is time to mimic the lion characteristics of our Lord and Savior Jesus Christ, declaring the Word of God with strength and power, expecting the manifestation of God's promises. For a life-changing experience read on.

FOREWORD

Behold, the Lion of the tribe of Judah...has prevailed.

—REVELATION 5:5

In life we search for answers to our deepest desires and fears, wondering if there will ever be a day that victory will be proclaimed in every area of our lives. So often we search for such answers in our churches, pastors, spiritual superstars, and even exploring avenues of the world, hoping and praying the void we feel will finally be filled, or perhaps just disappear. Is there a missing truth to this journey of life that finds so many of us searching but never finding our true calling or purpose? Is it because we choose to settle for second best, allowing the enemy of this world to cause havoc in our lives? We constantly ask: Has all power really been given to me? Will there ever be sustaining peace in my life? Can I have victory in every area of my life? Will I see the goodness of the Lord in the land of the living? Is there any justice for all I have gone through? Can I truly have my heart's desire?

The answer to each of these questions is yes,

because the same power that raised Jesus from the dead really does live inside each one of us.

> But if the Spirit of Him who raised Jesus from the dead dwells in you, He who raised Christ from the dead will also give life to your mortal bodies through His Spirit who dwells in you.
> —Romans 8:11

Often such scriptures identifying our authority in God are just read, overlooked, and never believed. If access to the same power that raised Jesus from the dead lives within us then why are we still struggling to find our identity? Why are we living from paycheck to paycheck? Why do we feel incomplete? Of course, the whys continue and continue and continue, leaving us restless and unfulfilled.

Our world is framed by the words we speak. Death and life are in the power of the tongue. (See Proverbs 18:21.) Unfortunately, not much life is being spoken these days, because circumstances deem us not to. The light bulb has to come on sooner or later when we will understand that we really do have the power to obtain everything we need on this earth through what we speak from our mouths. In fact, most of us go through life not speaking much of anything, because we are wishing and hoping that some day it will get better. Not! The words we speak are to be echoes of praise proclaiming the Word of God in every circumstance, demanding a change, and not letting go just as Jacob did until the change was manifested.

Who is Jacob and what can we learn from him? Jacob was the son of Isaac who had twelve sons, who established the twelve tribes of Israel. In Genesis 32:25–28 Jacob decided he was tired of life the way it was and needed things to change. Through his persistence God answered his prayers. Jacob understood that what he needed could only come from God and he was willing to fight for it, no matter how long it took. Sure enough his prayers were answered. He saw God face to face and everything changed, including his name.

In the presence of God everything changes, but we fail to realize that it may not come as easily as we would think, hope, or prefer. With so many demands and deadlines, our focus is often hindered and fixated on irrelevant things compared to experiencing the presence of God. Loneliness, depression, lack of resources, demanding spouses, crying children, weird church people—all distractions from the One who can change it all.

So, how can we bypass the distractions and unanswered questions to experience a life of victory? The answer may seem shocking, but it is time to fight. There is a lion in all of us who needs to be awakened to roar the oracles of the Most High God and *demand change and victory!*

> But one of the elders said to me, "Do not weep. Behold, the Lion of the tribe of Judah, the Root of David, has prevailed to open the scroll and to loose its seven seals."
>
> —REVELATION 5:5

We know Jesus as the Lamb of God who takes away the sins of the world, but do we know His brave warrior side with superior strength, courage, fearlessness, and voraciousness in destroying the works of the devil? The Lion of the tribe of Judah speaks volumes to every believer, telling us that we have access to the power and boldness to proclaim His Word from our mouths and achieve victory over every circumstance.

Nothing in life is free or comes without hard work, and it is time Christians understand this fact. Marriages can be restored, singles can marry a proper mate, wealth can be obtained, and peace of mind can be maintained once we do. But there is an enemy working overtime making sure such requests and heart's desires never come to pass. Pause for a moment and think about this. If the devil is working overtime, then why aren't Christians working overtime? We are barely praying, never reading the Bible, and the idea of pronouncing or roaring forth the Word of God over our circumstance is as distant from our daily living as the East is from the West.

There is a difference between knowing about God and really experiencing His Word coming alive with action in our lives. To experience the Word of God we must come to the realization that we must awaken the Lion of Judah inside each of us. Not tomorrow, but today. We must open our mouths and literally roar the Word of God over our marriages, singleness, wealthy places, minds, and every area that concerns us. There is power in prayer and praise when we strategically speak the Word of God and declare to every demon in hell, "I have the victory and I will not shut my mouth until I receive what I need from the Lord," just as Jacob did. (See Genesis 32:26.)

If Jesus is described throughout Scripture as a Lion, then we should want to be just like Him, displaying characteristics such as strength, courage, confidence, fearlessness, and voraciousness in destroying the works of our adversary. Such characteristics mimicked in the lives of a handful of believers would cause a revolution. Maybe a new tribe of Judah or remnant thereof could arise, turn the tables on the enemy, and wreak havoc on the kingdom of darkness instead of allowing the havoc in our own lives. There is a lion inside us—when it is awakened, the entire world will know the Lion of the tribe of Judah is real and nothing will ever again be missing in the life of the believer.

In this book we will look at the characteristics of the Lion, as well as explore the history of the tribe of Judah and how it relates to us as believers today. Prepare yourself for a life-changing experience!

☙ 1 ❧

JESUS, MY STRENGTH

> A lion...is mighty among beasts and does not
> turn away from any.
> —PROVERBS 30:30

The strength of a lion is superior to all other
beasts of the jungle. Lions understand their
strength, and when prey is caught there is no letting go. The strength of a lion is unquenchable, and
nothing can tell the beast otherwise. Lions mature
in their strength daily, because of the need to protect their young and capture enough prey or food to
survive. So, what if the lion never exercised its God-
given strength? Could the lion and cubs survive? As
we know, the lion and cubs would eventually die
because they need food to live just as believers need
the Bible to survive this sin-sick world.

> The old lion perishes for lack of prey, and the
> cubs of the lioness are scattered.
> —JOB 4:11

Without the Word of God becoming alive in our
everyday lives, we too will perish like the lion without

7

prey. Unfortunately, our lack of feeding on the Bible affects us, not only personally, but also everything around us, including our families, churches, and the world we live in. As the whelps or young cubs are forced to wander hopelessly about looking for food, so do our families, churches, and world wander for direction, all because we fail to know and share the Word of God.

> The Lord will give strength to his people; the Lord will bless his people with peace.
>
> —PSALM 29:11

Since Jesus is the Lion of Judah, we must embrace His impeccable strength displayed in the Bible. Only then can we fulfill the purpose for which He redeemed us and do the impossible.

> Finally, my brethren, be strong in the Lord and in the power of his might.
>
> —EPHESIANS 6:10

Paul realized he needed the same tenacity to stand against the devil as the lion seeking food for its cubs. Such strength could only come from the Lord.

There is strength in knowing the Word of God because it becomes our life instead of mere, lifeless words on a page. We begin to understand that we cannot live this life without the strength of the Lord. It is impossible! So, stop trying and start sharing this truth with your families, churches, and the world. To live day-to-day without fully embracing the strength of the Lord is as unwise as withholding nourishment to live from the body.

> A wise man is strong, yes, a man of knowledge increaseth strength.
>
> —PROVERBS 24:5

We must realize that strength cannot be found in plastic surgery, brain stimulants, prescription drugs, overeating, or riches, but only in the Lord and through knowing the Bible. Our appetites will never be tamed and minds never settled until the strength of the Lord is utilized. Even experiencing burnout or constant fatigue is a sign that we are relying on our own strength and not the strength of the Lord. To rely on the strength of the Lord is to speak—roar—what the Bible says about times of weakness or distress. Pause for a moment and mediate on the following passages of Scripture:

> For the joy of the LORD is your strength.
>
> —NEHEMIAH 8:10

> O LORD, my strength and my Redeemer.
>
> —PSALM 19:14

> But the salvation of the righteous is from the LORD; He is their strength in the time of trouble.
>
> —PSALM 37:39

> Seek the LORD and His strength; Seek His face evermore.
>
> —1 CHRONICLES 16:11

> The LORD is my strength and song, and He has become my salvation.
>
> —PSALM 118:14

If your heart is racing, or if tears are rolling down your face, then maybe you are finally accepting the fact that you cannot face life's challenges by yourself. God wants to be your strength, but He will not force you to understand this truth. God hears our prayers, understands our needs, and wants to show Himself strong on our behalf.

> Now I know that the LORD saves His anointed; He will answer him from His holy heaven With the saving strength of His right hand.
>
> —PSALM 20:6

God delivered the Israelites from Egypt. In Exodus 13, Moses reiterated three times:

> By strength of hand the LORD brought us out of Egypt, out of the house of bondage.
> —EXODUS 13:14

God also delivered David from Saul and his enemies, and David responded in praise in Psalm 18 and acknowledged the Lord as his strength. In 2 Timothy 4:17, Paul said the Lord stood with him and strengthened him as he preached to the Gentiles. Imagine what life-changing experiences can occur when we rise up as lions, declaring into the atmosphere the strength we have in the Lion of Judah, proclaimed through the Word of God:

> The LORD, is my strength and song; He also has become my salvation.
> —ISAIAH 12:2

The Hebrew word *owz* means "strength, force, security, majesty, or praise." Visualizing the Lord as a force means believing He is strong enough to bear our weaknesses—so let Him. He is our security blanket. When relationships fall apart He is dependable—so depend on Him. Above all else, He is absolute perfection, spectacular in power, and indeed worthy of all glory and honor; praise Him.

Relying on the strength of the Lord makes life so much easier, because we can now rest in the reality of who Jesus is; our strength. It is about time we all rest and trust in the Lord, for worrying never solves anything. Besides, less worrying means less wrinkles. (Now *that* is a cool bumper sticker idea!)

> Trust in the LORD forever, For in YAH, the LORD, is everlasting strength.
>
> —ISAIAH 26:4

Jacob obviously relied on the strength of the Lord. When wrestling with the angel he did not let go until he received his blessing, just as lions will not let go of their prey or food once captured. Therefore, we must hold on to our dreams, visions, and aspirations until they manifest.

> For the vision is yet for an appointed time; But at the end it will speak, and it will not lie. Though it tarries, wait for it; Because it will surely come, It will not tarry.
>
> —HABAKKUK 2:3

This scripture verse encourages us, but one word seems to suggest some uneasiness: *tarry*, which suggests perseverance and abiding. Why does the vision have to tarry and for how long?

The vision tarries because that is part of the process. We know where we want to be, but God simply says, *Not yet!* We want to work in the area of our gifts and callings. We want to get married, or have a great marriage, or have disciplined children. We want to attend a church where the Holy Spirit is free to change man's plans. We want to live debt free. We want to walk away from an unfulfilling job and work full time utilizing our God-given gifts and talents. Such wants are OK, because God himself inspires them. However, before we can obtain all these wants, there is a process we all must go through. This process births a *lifestyle* of prayer, fasting, praise, worship, and knowing the Word of God with full reliance on no one but God.

> But those who wait on the LORD Shall renew their strength; They shall mount up with wings like eagles, they shall run and not be weary, They shall walk and not faint.
> —ISAIAH 40:31

God is molding us into His image to strengthen and help us, which is why we must rely on His strength and not our own. Even when we feel the urge to be impatient—trying to make things happen for ourselves—we must stop and go back to what the Bible says.

> Fear not, for I am with you; Be not dismayed, for I am your God. I will strengthen you, Yes, I will help you, I will uphold you with My righteous right hand.
>
> —ISAIAH 41:10

Since there is no use in fighting this process in which God forms our character, habits, and thoughts, simply allow Him to be your strength. Through what seems like the hardest times of our lives, God says *I will strengthen the house of Judah.* (See Zechariah 10:6.) Strength comes from declaring the praises of God as brave lions full of His strength and demanding every hindrance to bow at the feet of Jesus.

Though the vision tarries, it shall come to pass and all our dreams will come true. Until then, we must be diligent to roar the Word of God.

> But may the God of all grace, who called us to His eternal glory by Christ Jesus, after you have suffered a while, perfect, establish, strengthen, and settle you.
>
> —1 PETER 5:10

WAR PRAYER FOR STRENGTH

Lord, search my heart and take out everything that is not like You. Lamb of God, forgive me for all my sins. I thank You for Your precious blood, which covers me. Create in me a clean heart.

Lion of Judah, show Yourself strong on my behalf. I declare that You are my strength and my song. Lord, I trust in Your strength today to deal with (_____ name your circumstance). Wherever I am weak, Lord please be my strength. Depression, I command you to go to the feet of Jesus. Negative thoughts, I command you to go to the feet of Jesus. Spirits of fatigue and hopelessness, I command you to go to the feet of Jesus. This day, the joy of the Lord is my strength, for "I can do all things through Christ who strengthens me" (Phil. 4:13). Lion of Judah, be my strength. Amen.

◎ 2 ◎

COURAGE, CONFIDENCE, AND FEARLESSNESS

> Where is the dwelling of the lions, And the feeding place of the young lions, Where the lion walked, the lioness and lion's cub, and no one made them afraid?
>
> —NAHUM 2:11

Lions are brave, fearless beasts. If the slightest flinch of fear is sensed, the lion's reputation as the strongest and bravest beast of the jungle is diminished. Therefore, lions have to be brave. Prey is not just going to fall at their feet; the lion has to be strong and courageous in finding and capturing enough food for its cubs, as well as to protect them.

The scripture passage in Nahum 2:11 can be viewed as an example of the lion's fearlessness, showing us that we must also establish such a reputation.

What are courage, confidence, and fearlessness? Well, courage is believing God when we stop believing in ourselves. Confidence is knowing that God loves us and has our back, regardless if we fail or succeed. Fearlessness is believing the Word of God despite how bad the situation looks.

Establishing a reputation of fearlessness against our adversary the devil can only cause havoc to the kingdom of darkness, and it's about time we stop putting up with the enemy's foolishness, anyway. To be defiant in the face of adversity sends a message of confidence that we know in whom we believe. For our only fear as believers ought to be for the Lord and no one else. (See Proverbs 9:10.)

Having a reputation that allows no hindrances from the devil is crucial to the Christian walk but unfortunately the average believer is coasting hopelessly with his or her mouth shut as the enemy destroys everything around them. Believers must rise from their slumber and declare from their mouths that the enemy of this world cannot have our marriages, children, loved ones, churches, or country. The Bible says we are more than conquerors. (See Romans 8:37.) No weapon formed against us shall prosper. (See Isaiah 54:17.) Our conclusion? Victory is eminent!

With so many dreams and visions yet to be birthed, we must be confident that God is ready to bring to pass our hearts' desires. As a result, fear and doubt can no longer be a part of the life of a believer and nowhere near our thoughts. It is time to awaken the Lion of Judah within us, and declare the Word of God in strength and in power, devoid of fear.

No longer can the tactics and hindrances of the devil move us, because the light bulb is now coming on and we understand that our strength comes from the Lord. This truth makes us courageous, confident and so *unstoppable*.

> For I, the LORD your God, will hold your right hand, Saying to you, "Fear not; I will help you."
> —ISAIAH 41:13

Who dares to whisper lies of defeat and hopelessness in the ear of the believer when the same power that raised Jesus from the dead lives inside each of us, making us weapons of mass destruction against the enemy? Dream snatchers, negative words, and gift blockers cannot hinder our progress. There is too much at stake to even be bothered by crazy family members, jealous church people, and silly co-workers when destiny and our wealthy place are in reach.

The devil roams around like a lion seeking whom he may devour. (See 1 Peter 5:8.) The scripture says *like* a lion, meaning the devil is an imitator and a big fake, whose bark is bigger than his bite. Our roar of praise declaring our confidence and fearlessness through the Word of God overshadows and destroys the bark of the enemy.

> But the righteous are bold as a lion.
> —Proverbs 28:1

Indeed, we as believers are to be as bold as a lion—and not just any lion, but a lion full of strength, confidence, and fearlessness, no longer putting up with junk from the enemy.

> You must not fear them, for the Lord your God Himself fights for you.
> —Deuteronomy 3:22

> The Lord is my light and my salvation; Whom shall I fear? The Lord is the strength of my life; Of whom shall I be afraid?
> —Psalm 27:1

> In the fear of the Lord there is strong confidence, And His children will have a place of refuge.
> —Proverbs 14:26

> For God hath not given us a spirit of fear, but of power and of love and of a sound mind.
> —2 Timothy 1:7

> So we may boldly say: "The Lord is my helper; I will not fear. What can man do to me?"
> —Hebrews 13:6

Life as we know it changes when our trust is placed in the Lord instead of ourselves. In Genesis 15:1 God told Abraham not to fear, for He will be his shield and exceeding great reward. As we are obedient to the plan of God, meaning trusting His process, we are protected from harm and the rewards are worth the process. Even if we were given everything our little hearts desired, but our confidence and fearlessness were never developed, could we hold on to it? Probably not, because if we never practice exercising our authority in Christ, then the enemy will continue to steal from us and play havoc with our lives. The pattern of defeat and unbelief will be a vicious cycle that would last for generations:

> Look, the LORD your God has set the land before you; go up and possess it, as the LORD God of you fathers has spoken to you; do not fear or be discouraged.
> —DEUTERONOMY 1:21

Moses had a huge responsibility in leading the Israelites into the Promised Land, but they encountered a process as well, which developed their courage and confidence in the Lord and eventually a manifested promise. More importantly, while going through the process Moses was able to experience the glory of God as he hid in the cleft of the rock.

Experiencing the presence of God is worth going through any process, because nowhere else but from the Lord can we find strength and courage. As Jacob and Moses encountered and as we are learning, everything leads back to the feet of Jesus. Jesus is superior in strength and He is our example of courage, confidence, and fearlessness. This truth realized in every believer will force the enemy to think twice about messing with our dreams, our families, and our churches.

> Now this is the confidence that we have in Him, that if we ask anything according to His will, He hears us. And if we know that He hears us, whatever we ask, we know that we have the petitions that we have asked of Him.
>
> —1 JOHN 5:14–15

Asking anything according to His will gives us the assurance that nothing is impossible with God. There is meaning to life and through God we can accomplish His will. Why feel discouraged when there is freedom in declaring the Word of God? Being betrayed by our silence is no longer a figure of speech, but a reality if we fail to dominate our environment with the Bible. (See Luke 14:34–35.) God's Word speaks life into our inner man giving us strength, confidence, and wisdom to demand change all around us. Addictions of any sort are no challenge when the Word of God comes alive and is spoken with conviction and authority.

Our responsibility as believers is to declare the Word of God even when we do not feel like it. We have no choice but to roar His Word through sleepless nights, stressful work hours, painful moments with backbiting church members, cheating spouses, rebellious children, and all the other mad issues of life. Victory is for every believer who dares to declare the Word of God indefinitely, even after the promise is manifested. So, until Jesus—our Lion of Judah—officially gives the devil his long-awaited beat down, we must stand on the promises of the Bible. Shout unto God with a voice of triumph— for nothing less than victory is expected.

WAR PRAYER FOR COURAGE, CONFIDENCE, AND FEARLESSNESS

Lord, search my heart and take out everything that is not like You. Lamb of God, forgive me for all my sins. I thank You for Your precious blood, which covers me. Create in me a clean heart.

This day, I declare victory in every area of my life. Satan, I command you to leave my (_____ list all areas) in the name of Jesus. I am confident in whom I believe, because the same power that raised Jesus from the dead lives in me. Therefore, I exercise my authority through the blood and name of Jesus. Let Your will be done in me, oh Lord. Have Your way in me. Fear, I command you to bow at the feet of Jesus. Doubt and unbelief, I command you to bow at the feet of Jesus. Low self-esteem, I command you to bow at the feet of Jesus.

I am more than a conqueror and I fear no one but God. Lion of Judah, rise within me. Show Yourself strong on my behalf. You are superior in strength. You are courageous. You are my confidence. You are fearless, therefore I am fearless. Lion of Judah, reign in me this day in Jesus' name. Amen.

◎ 3 ◎

ATTACK FIRST

As a lion is eager to tear his prey, And like a young lion lurking in secret places.
—PSALM 17:12

Lions are voracious. They are greedy and eager to devour. They lurk in secret places ready to devour their prey. When lions are hungry they are ready to eat and nothing will stop them. They will use their strength and fearlessness to get what they want. However, their tactics of capturing prey are done by secretly waiting or hiding for the right time or opportunity to attack. Lions are often on the offensive rather than on the defensive, because they want to attack first.

Comprehending the voracious character of a lion permeates a spiritual stance that is missing in the life of the believer, because to embrace such a stance forces us to be on the offensive rather than on the defensive. To be on the offense allows us to prepare ourselves in secret through prayer, fasting, and reading the Bible, to know ahead of time what the enemy is planning against the will of the Lord for our lives.

The enemy secretly lies in wait like a lion in his

den waiting to catch his prey (Ps. 10:9). The very idea that the enemy is secretly finding ways to destroy marriages, hinder callings, and misdirect churches, should infuriate every believer. How can the enemy cause havoc in our lives without our knowing it? The devil is a liar!

The truth is being revealed. No longer will we see our dreams as hindered and unattainable. From all walks of life we must become enraged with what the enemy is doing around us. This rage should force us to become eager with a vicious, greedy appetite to bind the works of the devil.

> And whatever you bind on earth will be bound in heaven.
>
> —MATTHEW 16:19

We have the strength and fearlessness to attack first by circumventing the enemy's plans through proclaiming the Word of God as loud as we can through prayer and praise. What a powerful truth to know that we can be on the offensive and curtail the plans of the enemy through the Word of God.

> Lest Satan should take advantage of us; for we are not ignorant of his devices.
>
> —2 CORINTHIANS 2:11

God in His infinite wisdom made man in His image, giving us all we need to live a life of victory and wholeness. Therefore, our guard must remain up and our spirits sharp to discern the plans of the enemy. As the lion lies in secret, waiting and studying its prey, we too must have our spiritual antennae in position at all times to know when the enemy is attempting to destroy our minds, children, spouses, or spiritual leaders.

Take a moment and examine the times in your life when in a split second the Holy Spirit brought someone or something across your mind or path and you failed to stop and pray. Oh, the familiar words we hear over and over again, "I'll be praying for you." This spirit of laziness and self-absorption is unacceptable when lives are at stake and suicide is an alternative.

Have our lives become so busy that we cannot even intercept the plans of the enemy for others and ourselves? Reality check—until we awaken the Lion of Judah within ourselves, the enemy will continue making our lives miserable. So, what will you do?

In Psalm 58:6, David was able to discern the plans of the enemy when he cried out to God to break their teeth. David knew that if the teeth of his enemy were destroyed then it would be impossible for them to devour him. In Psalm 58:6, the reference to the word *teeth* comes from the Hebrew words *shen* or *shanan*, which means "to pierce, sharpen, or teach diligently." We know that lions use their teeth to devour their prey just as the enemy of this world deploys fiery darts of lies and mistruths to kill our hopes and dreams. So, what should the believer be using to devour the enemy of this world? The "teeth of the believer" is metaphorical for the Word of God.

> For the word of God is living and powerful, and sharper than any two-edged sword, piercing even to the division of soul and spirit, and of the joints and marrow, and is a discerner of the thoughts and intents of the heart.
>
> —HEBREWS 4:12

The Bible declared from our mouth devours the plans of the enemy as it cuts and pierces through the darkness to enlighten our hearts and minds giving us rest from all distress.

> Your word I have hidden in my heart, That I might not sin against You.
>
> —PSALM 119:11

> Your word is a lamp to my feet and a light to my path.
>
> —PSALM 119:105

Forever, O LORD, Your word is settled in
heaven.

—PSALM 119:89

For my mouth will speak truth; Wickedness
is an abomination to my lips.

—PROVERBS 8:7

As the teeth of the lion are sharp, so is the infallible Word of God. Therefore, we must learn to awaken the Lion of Judah within us to attack first with God's Word. The answers to life's questions and circumstances are found in the Word of God, allowing us to experience heaven on earth and a chance to breathe free. (See John 8:32.)

If we fail to open our mouths and declare God's Word with conviction and authority, we cannot expect to devour the enemy of lack, sickness, loneliness, low self-esteem, betrayal, or unforgiveness. We must use our teeth and voraciously be on guard to intercept the plans of the enemy through roaring the Word of God and accepting nothing less than total victory in every area of our life.

Let the high praises of God be in their mouth,
And a two-edged sword in their hand.

—PSALM 149:6

The God we serve should be an appealing force in the world if our lives mimic victory and not defeat. Who wants to serve a God with a record of defeat, anyway? The greater One lives inside of us, and every believer must awaken the Lion of Judah within. The world awaits such victory and an opportunity to be free.

When we arise from self-absorption to roar the Word of God, everything around us changes, including our world. In case you did not know, we live not just for ourselves, but that others who do not know Christ will want to know him as well. Romans 8 reminds us that not only are the believers waiting for the sons of God to be manifested, but the world as well. There is a desire in every human being to be like our Creator. Instead of celebrities dictating culture, believers must rise up and set the standard. This standard honors God by relying on His wisdom, making Him proud that we are His children.

God loves us and wants nothing less than the best for us, but He is bound by His Word. His Word, realized and lived, renders freedom to be everything He created us to be. This is why the enemy sends roadblocks and distractions to keep us from knowing the Bible and makes it difficult to declare it.

When the Word of God is hidden in our hearts and echoed from our mouths we become part of a remnant of the tribe of Judah, which recognizes who they are in Christ with all impossibilities becoming possible.

> And the remnant of Jacob Shall be among the Gentiles, In the midst of many peoples, Like a lion among the beasts of the forest, Like a young lion among flocks of sheep, Who, if he passes through, Both treads down and tears in pieces, And none can deliver.
>
> —MICAH 5:8

This special remnant has the appetite of a lion and is willing to fulfill their purpose in the earth, ensuring havoc to the kingdom of darkness. If called to write, this remnant will publish. If called to sing, they will record. If called to mother, they will nurture. If called to preach, they will teach. If called to minister internationally, they will witness. If called to pastor, they will serve. If called to wealth, they will give and start their own companies. The world takes risks, but the just live by faith. (See Romans 1:17.)

The time is now for every believer to take their rightful place in their God-given callings. Roar the Word of God with strength, courage, confidence, fearlessness, and voraciousness, expecting all things to be possible according to the will of God. (See Philippians 4:13.)

WAR PRAYER FOR ATTACKING FIRST

Lord, please search my heart and take out everything that is not like You. Lamb of God, forgive me for all my sins. I thank You for Your precious blood, which covers me. Create in me a clean heart.

I am a lion in the tribe of Judah, roaring the Word of God over my (_____ list areas of concern), roaring praises to the Most High God, and giving Jesus the glory and honor He rightfully deserves. I am empowered by the strength of the Lord. I am courageous and fearless, declaring victory in every area of my life. I am not ignorant of the enemy's plans and devices. Therefore, I stand guard over my destiny, my purpose, my ministry, my family, and my church through the Word of God.

The greater One lives inside of me. I am more than a conqueror. With God, all things are possible. By the stripes of Jesus I am healed. My family will live and not die and declare the works of the Lord. My God perfects that which concerns me. I am fearfully and wonderfully made, declaring that God will get the glory from my life. The Lion of Judah is awake within me and I declare triumph over every circumstance this day in Jesus' name. Procrastination, I command you to bow at the feet of Jesus. Self-absorption, I command you to bow at the feet of Jesus. Hopelessness, I command you to bow at the feet of Jesus. Lion of Judah, roar in me as I fulfill Your will in the earth this day. Amen.

THE LION OF JUDAH

> But one of the elders said to me, "Do not
> weep. Behold, the Lion of the tribe of Judah,
> the Root of David, has prevailed to open the
> scroll and to loose its seven seals."
>
> —REVELATION 5:5

Our first and ultimate example of strength, courage, confidence, fearlessness, and voraciousness in destroying the plans of the enemy is Jesus, the Lion of Judah. His very essence pronounces victory and assures us that in the end, we win.

The tribe of Judah consisted of strong and courageous warriors of praise who used their mouths and hands to war as lions. Even though Jesus' bloodline consisted of Abraham, Isaac, and Jacob He wanted to be identified as a lion and this reputation could be maintained within the tribe of Judah.

The Greek word for Judah in Revelation 5:5 is *Ioudas*, which comes from the Hebrew words *yehuwdah* and *yadah,* meaning to celebrate, to use the hands, to cast or throw stone or arrow at or away, to revere or worship with extended hands, to wring the hands, to confess, to praise, and to give thanks.

The hands and feet of Jesus were nailed to the cross. Stones were thrown at him and the government washed their hands of their guilt. Satan thought he had won, but God, to Satan's dismay, resurrected Jesus with all power. He conquered death, hell, and the grave, thereby signifying to the world that Satan could not tie his hands or feet, and the stones thrown at Jesus would be thrown right back at Satan through our praise and worshiping of the King of kings and Lord of lords.

Jesus sprang out of Judah. (See Hebrews 7:14.) Being a part of the tribe of Judah confirms that prayer, praise, and worship are crucial elements in defeating the enemy and living a more abundant life. (See John 10:10.) As the Word of God is confessed—or roared—we celebrate victory over every circumstance.

With our hands raised, we give honor to the Most High God, while at the same time disrupting the enemy's plans. As we pray, praise, and worship, darts and arrows are thrown to confuse and destroy the enemy, causing the havoc he so deserves. It is obvious that we are in a war, but when we utilize our weapons of mass destruction we become like Jesus—invincible against the plans of Satan. The Lord is our strength and He teaches our hands to war and our fingers to fight. (See Psalm 144:1.)

In Genesis 33, Moses blessed Judah saying let his *hands* be sufficient for him and be a help against the enemy. In Numbers the tribe of Judah was the largest of the twelve tribes of Israel and the first to depart Sinai. They often were leaders in everything from offering their tithes, dividing land, and blessing the people, to entering into battle against the Canaanites and Benjamites.

David was part of the tribe of Judah and he defeated Goliath when everyone else was running scared. He used his hand and killed the Philistine. (See 1 Samuel 17:49.) Before Goliath, he rescued one of his lambs from the teeth of a lion—poor lion did not even know what hit him. David used his hands to war, and was eventually anointed king over the house of Judah. Through life experiences he produced the many war praises in the book of Psalms. Lest we forget, David was a man after God's own heart.

There are many examples of the lion's strength and fearlessness represented by the tribe of Judah throughout scripture. These examples serve to inspire us to be all that God has called us to be and to imitate Jesus, our ultimate example. Jacob prophesied in Genesis 49 that his son Judah would be the one his brothers will praise.

> Judah is a lion's whelp...who shall rouse him?
> The scepter shall not depart from Judah, Nor
> a lawgiver from between his feet, Until Shi-
> loh comes.
>
> —GENESIS 49:9–10

As Jacob describes Judah, he also foreshadows the Messiah to come through his son's tribe. The Hebrew word for scepter is *shebet*, meaning branch or stick for punishing. As Jacob reminds us to not let go until we receive our blessing, he informs us in Genesis 49 to awake the Lion of Judah within us and fight with sticks or implements of prayer, praise, and worship until Jesus returns. Being entrusted with such insight concerning events that would take place centuries later is mind-boggling.

Micah also prophesied that among the thousands:

> "[One] shall come forth...Whose goings
> forth are from of old, From everlast-
> ing...He shall be great To the ends of the
> earth" (Mic. 5:2, 4).

> "He shall have dominion also from sea to
> sea, And from the River to the ends of
> the earth" (Ps. 72:8).

"He shall speak peace to the nations" (Zech. 9:10).

"He will be great...of His kingdom there will be no end" (Luke 1:32–33).

Jesus is our guide, fulfilling our calling and purpose in the earth. Since He is great, we are great. Since He has dominion, we walk in that same authority of His Word, expecting peace all around us. Since he reigns, we reign in victory over every circumstance.

Jesus is perfection and the reason why we live. His sacrifice of enduring such a painful and horrific death allows us to live a life of victory. To live anything less causes His dying to be in vain. Therefore, we owe Jesus nothing less than to represent Him in the earth as brave lions declaring the Word of God with strength, courage, confidence, and fearlessness, and with appetites to destroy the plans of the devil.

Jesus is described not just as the Lamb of God, but as the Lion of Judah—equipped to accomplish the will of His Father with authority and conviction.

☙ 5 ❧

It Is Time to Roar

Their voice shall roar like the sea.
—Jeremiah 50:42

Obtaining strength, courage, confidence, fearlessness, and an appetite to intercept the plans of the enemy results from knowing the Bible and letting it roar with consistency. Even if the Bible is not yet rooted in the heart it will be, once spoken. The key is to roar—and roar we shall!

When a lion roars, terror invades the jungle. Everything and everyone who hears its sound is petrified. The sound of the roar spreads such fear that the lion can proceed to take or destroy whatever it chooses with no questions asked. The lion's strength and fearlessness are consistent and cannot be challenged. Lions roar after their prey and seize whatever they desire. (See Psalm 104:21.)

Imagine if we maintained a consistent stance like the lion to roar the Word of God demanding our loved ones to be saved:

> Demanding wholeness and respect within
> our marriages

Demanding obedience and self-discipline
   from our children

Demanding our churches to allow the presence of God to flow

Demanding our bodies to be healed and
   disciplined lifestyles to follow

Demanding our true callings to be manifested according to the will of God

Demanding that every man, woman, boy,
   and girl in all seven continents have the
   opportunity to know Jesus

Demanding every promise in His Word be
   experienced

Today, there is a roar being heard across the
land. It is the sound of the tribe of Judah becoming
enraged with what the enemy has been allowed to
do uncontested for too long. God's Word is begin-
ning to be roared with strength and fearlessness
day and night. Not only is this sound petrifying
the devil, but the God of Creation is listening.
Watch out! God hears the cry of the righteous
and when He hears His Word spoken, He watches

over it to perform it. (See Jeremiah 1:12.) Therefore, consider it done.

Hannah cried out to God and her desire to be a mother was manifested. Daniel needed to be rescued from death and God delivered him upon hearing his request. Esther had to speak up or her entire nation would have been destroyed. The men of Israel and Judah were able to defeat the Philistines, but not without a shout first. David not only spoke the Word, but wrote it while Saul pronounced a death sentence on him. Deborah sang praises to the Lord in the midst of sin and idolatry. Gideon and the children of Israel defeated the Midianites after the Lord heard their cry. The woman with the issue of blood was healed after she captured the attention of Jesus by touching Him with her hand.

> In the beginning was the Word, and the Word was with God, and the Word was God.
> —JOHN 1:1

Jesus—the Lamb of God, the Lion of Judah— came to earth to redeem man back to God, and to illustrate how to live by the Word of God. Scripture was fulfilled in Matthew 26:56 when Jesus endured the journey of the cross.

> I do not seek My own will but the will of the
> Father who sent Me.
>
> —JOHN 5:30

As with Jesus and the many servants of the Bible, the journey of life requires us to know and speak the Word of God. We must rely on His Word, establishing a reputation of frightening the enemy. The truth of the matter is, our lives will never be the same until our habits emulate the character of Christ.

> They shall walk after the LORD. He will roar
> like a lion. When He roars, Then His sons
> shall come trembling from the west
>
> —HOSEA 11:10

The Hebrew term for the word *roar* is *shag*, meaning to mourn or rumble mightily. Jesus roared, therefore we must roar. In fact, the cute and oh-so-sophisticated among us have been escorted from the building, and those wanting a change from the norm are ready for God to move and shake up everything around them.

We are no longer afraid of the roar of the enemy (see Isaiah 31:4), because our roar is louder and it is the mighty Word of God. The Lion of Judah will protect and deliver His people. We not only expect change, we demand it. The key is being persistent in our roaring, because the moment we stop is when the enemy will throw his darts of confusion and depression.

This truth being revealed is causing a revolution in the body of Christ and a remnant is forming who are firm in whom they believe. This remnant is roaring the Word of God with strength, courage, confidence, fearlessness, and an appetite of rage, destroying the plans of the enemy over our lives, our communities, our schools, our churches, and our world.

WHAT REALLY MATTERS

In Your presence is fullness of joy; At Your
right hand are pleasures forevermore.
— PSALM 16:11

Salaries increase, houses enlarge, friendships
develop, families grow, and churches build—but
it all means nothing without the presence of
God. His presence makes the difference as it
brings strength, courage, and peace to our lives,
but sadly it is often the missing factor in the life
of the believer. Our spirits are unsettled and our
minds are still on the freeway long after we arrive
home, because we have not seized every opportunity to roar in praise and pray the Word of God.
If we are true followers of Christ, we must represent Him well in the earth. Circumstances can no
longer dictate the course of our lives. The same
power that raised Jesus from the dead lives inside
each of us—the time is now to awaken the Lion
of Judah to stand as fearless lions expecting the
promises of God to be experienced.

Jesus is soon to come and there are many souls
still to be saved, but first we must get ourselves

together by personally knowing and experiencing the Bible. Although time is running out, God is ready to do what we believe in His Word to do.

His will for our lives has become a mandate, leaving no time for excuses. Dreams must be moved from the mind and manifested, because dreams lined with the will of God are to be fulfilled. We must trust God even if it means leaving the security blanket of a job, family, or church. For the rewards of fulfilling your purpose in the earth is worth whatever consequences.

> But the just shall live by his faith.
> —HABAKKUK 2:4

As brave lions with the Word of God on our lips, being spoken with strength and confidence, there is nothing we cannot do. And there is nothing too hard for our God. (See Jeremiah 32:27.) God is on our side—we can do the impossible! Always remember, our purpose is not predicated on what people think, but on God's Word. For that reason, if your first attempt at fulfilling your dreams is hindered, keep trying. Your lion's appetite will accomplish the will of God regardless.

God wants us to rely on Him for absolutely everything, just as Jesus did. Jesus always kept His purpose in view and on His lips just as we must. He is our ultimate example:

> For the Son of Man has come to save that which was lost.
>
> —MATTHEW 18:11

The Word of God shapes us into His image allowing us to experience His presence while at the same time intercepting the plans of the enemy. There is only one God who can cover us like that. God wants to be invited into our world more frequently than just on Sundays or midweek Bible study. Learn to converse with Him throughout the day and even through the night. He is listening attentively and is ready to act according to the words spoken out of our mouths when the words He hears are His. Promises are manifested when the Word of God is spoken. Peace covers the mind and soundness returns. Rest in the promises of the Bible, for it sustains a victorious life.

The Lion of Judah must roar within us until He comes again and sends Satan and all his demons to the bottomless pit. (See Revelation 20:3.) Therefore, our prayer, praise, and worship must never stop. They invite the presence of God and ambush the plans of Satan. Yea!

There is a sound from the tribe of Judah being heard across the land, similar to falling rain. The Holy Spirit is being poured out as this remnant roars, demanding the will of God to be realized and experienced. Will you be a part of this remnant?

To God be the glory, who reigns in strength and power, creating masterpieces of Himself inside each and every one of us. Seeing that it was good, He went further to redeem us to Himself when man chose to disobey. God knew before we were born what He wanted us to accomplish in the earth, so He gave us Jesus. Through His word, He informed us to just do it. As a result, we are the standard.

> What is man that You are mindful of him...
> For You have made him a little lower than the
> angels.
>
> —PSALM 8:4-5

A God willing to ransom His only son for our sins—while giving us everything we need to live a life of wholeness and victory, eradicating life's issues and circumstances through His Word—is nothing short of amazing. Decide today to be all God has called you to be. Never stop until you hear Him tell you, "Well done, good and faithful servant" (Matt. 25:21). Be blessed as you allow the Lion of Judah

to roar in and through you this day, in Jesus' name.
Amen.

> Hear the sound of the Lion of Judah
> See the fire and the fear in the enemy's camp
> From the sound of the Lion of Judah roaring
> again
> There's a new generation arising
> A nameless, faceless, placeless tribe
> All they fear is the fear of the Lord
> All they hear is the Lion of Judah[1]

---

[1] "Lion of Judah," lyrics by Jason Upton, 40 Psalm Music/BMI © 2002. Used by permission.

To Contact the Author

Email: nandilyn@nandilyn.com

Web site: www.nandilyn.com